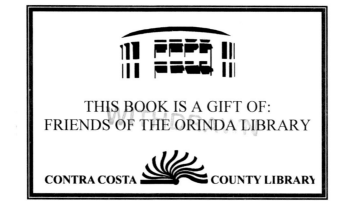

Origins of the Holocaust

David Downing

Please visit our web site at: www.worldalmanaclibrary.com
For a free color catalog describing World Almanac® Library's list of
high-quality books and multimedia programs, call 1-800-848-2928 (USA)
or 1-800-387-3178 (Canada). World Almanac® Library's fax: (414) 332-3567.

Library of Congress Cataloging-in-Publication Data

Downing, David, 1946-
    Origins of the Holocaust / by David Downing.
        p. cm. — (World Almanac Library of the Holocaust)
    Includes bibliographical references and index.
    ISBN 0-8368-5943-X (lib. bdg.)
    ISBN 0-8368-5950-2 (softcover)
    1. Holocaust, Jewish (1939-1945)—Causes—Juvenile literature. I. Title. II. Series.
    D804.34.D68 2005
    940.53'1811—dc22   2005042114

First published in 2006 by
World Almanac® Library
A Member of the WRC Media Family of Companies
330 West Olive Street, Suite 100
Milwaukee, WI 53212 USA

Produced by Discovery Books
Editors: Geoff Barker, Sabrina Crewe, and Jacqueline Gorman
Designer and page production: Sabine Beaupré
Photo researchers: Geoff Barker and Rachel Tisdale
Maps: Stefan Chabluk
Consultant: Ronald M. Smelser, Professor of Modern German History, University of Utah
World Almanac® Library editorial direction: Mark J. Sachner
World Almanac® Library editor: Alan Wachtel
World Almanac® Library art direction: Tammy West
World Almanac® Library production: Jessica Morris

Photo credits: cover: USHMM; title page: Mary Evans Picture Library; p. 5: Keystone/Getty Images;
p. 9: Topfoto.co.uk; p. 10: Mary Evans Picture Library; p. 13: Library of Congress; p. 14: Topfoto.co.uk;
p. 17: Mary Evans Picture Library; p. 19: Topfoto.co.uk; p. 20: Mary Evans Picture Library; p. 21: Mary
Evans Picture Library; p. 22: Bettmann/Corbis; p. 25: Three Lions/Getty Images; p. 26: Three Lions/
Getty Images; p. 27: Topfoto.co.uk; p. 28: Hulton Archive/Getty Images; p. 31: Mary Evans Picture
Library; p. 32: Keystone/Getty Images; p. 35: Mary Evans Picture Library; p. 37: Three Lions/Getty
Images; p. 38: Topfoto.co.uk; p. 41: Getty Images; p. 43: Three Lions/Getty Images.

Printed in Canada

1 2 3 4 5 6 7 8 9 09 08 07 06 05

Cover: Adolf Hitler, leader of Nazi Germany, poses in 1933 with members of the
Schutzstaffel, or SS, which was the Nazis' own army and security force.

Title page: In the early 1920s, Nazi leader Adolf Hitler wrote a book he called *Mein Kampf
(My Struggle)*. In it, he outlined his vision for Germany's future and expressed his hatred
of Jews. This was the British cover of the first volume of Hitler's book.

Contents

The Holocaust

The Murder of Millions

The word *holocaust* has a long history. In early times, it meant a burnt offering to the gods, and in the **Middle Ages**, a huge sacrifice or destruction. It still has this second meaning today, particularly when used to describe large-scale destruction by fire or nuclear weapons. But since the 1970s, the word has gained a new and specific meaning. Today, when people refer to the Holocaust—with a capital "H"—they mean the murder of approximately six million Jews by Nazi Germany and its **allies** during World War II.

This crime had deep historical roots. In predominantly Christian Europe, the Jews had always been considered a race apart and had often endured persecution for that reason. When governments or peoples wanted someone to blame for misfortune, they often picked on an innocent and helpless, Jewish minority.

In the early twentieth century, many Germans wanted some-one to blame for their defeat in World War I and the terrible economic hardship that followed. They, too, picked on the Jews in their midst—with ultimately horrific results. The Holocaust was ordered and organized by political leaders, carried out by thousands of their willing supporters, and allowed to happen by millions of ordinary people.

The scale of the crime is still hard to take in. To use a modern comparison, about three thousand people were killed in the **terrorist** attacks in the United States on September 11, 2001. Between June 1941 and March 1945, an average of four thousand European Jews were murdered every day.

These people were killed in a variety of ways. Some were left to starve, some to freeze. Many were worked to death in **labor camps**. More than one million were shot and buried in mass graves. Several million were gassed to death in specially built **extermination camps** such as Auschwitz and Treblinka.

The Persecution of the Jews

Jews were not the only victims of the Nazis. In fact, it is probable that the Nazis and their allies murdered at least five million other **civilians** before and during World War II. Their victims were killed for a variety of reasons: **communists** for their political opinions, **homosexuals** for their sexual orientation, people with mental disabilities for their supposed uselessness to society, **Gypsies** and Slavs for their supposed racial inferiority, and Russians, Poles, and other eastern Europeans because they happened to be in the Nazis' way.

The central crime in the Holocaust—the murder of millions of Jews—was a long time in the making. Most of the actual killing took place between 1941 and 1945, but the Jews of Germany were subject to intense persecution from the moment Adolf Hitler and his Nazi Party took power in 1933. That persecution was itself merely the latest in a series of persecutions stretching back over almost two thousand years, in which every nation of Europe had at some time played a part.

This book looks at the origins of the Holocaust, how Jews became the victims of **genocide**, and how an apparently civilized nation started on a path that led to the murder of millions.

When the British liberated the Bergen-Belsen prison camp in April 1945, they discovered this mass grave. The mostly Jewish victims had died of starvation or disease.

CHAPTER ONE

The Jews

No Accident

The Holocaust was not a historical accident. It did not simply "happen," like a bolt from the blue. For most of the previous two thousand years, the Jews of Europe had been persecuted with varying degrees of intensity by their non-Jewish neighbors. What created the hostility behind this **anti-Semitism**, and what kept it simmering for so many centuries?

The Jewish People

Understanding the roots of the Holocaust requires some knowledge of who the Jewish people are. Who exactly are the Jews? This is more difficult to answer than it might seem.

Are Jews people who believe in or practice the religion of **Judaism**? Many of them do, but many do not. Some believe in no religion at all.

Are the Jews a specific race? No, Jews may come from any racial background. Some talk of a Semitic race, but in reality there is no such thing: The word *Semitic* refers to a group of languages, which includes both Hebrew, the traditional language of the Jews, and Arabic.

Are the Jews a nation? Not in the usual sense. Nations usually share a common piece of territory, and, until the establishment of Israel in 1948, the Jews had no such land of their own. Most Jews have always seen themselves as belonging to the nation in which they live, whichever it might be. Jews in Germany before World War II, for instance, considered themselves to be German as well as Jewish.

Are the Jews a cultural group, a body of people who share a common diet, similar dress, the same tastes in art, and so on? In modern times, this was certainly true of eastern European Jews, who even shared a unique language, Yiddish. There have

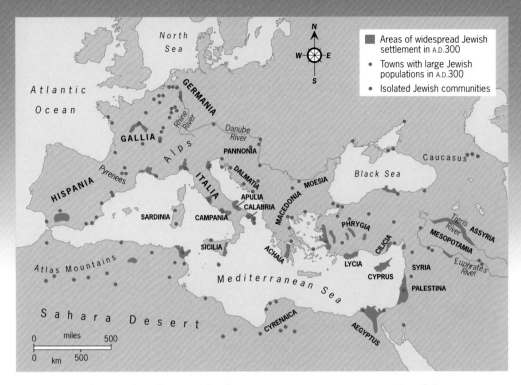

This map shows the dispersal of Jews across Europe, North Africa, and the Middle East between A.D. 100 and 300.

always been wide cultural differences, however, among the diverse Jewish communities that are found in different parts of the world.

Different groups of Jews can be connected in all, or some, or none of these ways. Perhaps the one thing that binds Jews together is their shared history—and the sense of themselves as a people that sharing that history gives them. Within that history, various factors, such as religious beliefs, language, food, music, literature, and art, have played key roles in bringing Jews together.

Jews and Christians

The first Jewish state was the Kingdom of Judah (or Judea), established in 922 B.C., in the West Bank territory now administered by Israel and the Palestinian Authority. This state was undermined by the Greeks and Babylonians and eventually taken over by the Romans. After a failed rebellion in A.D. 66–73, most Jews left the area, taking their faith and their cultural habits with them. They settled in small communities throughout the Roman Empire and even beyond. This scattering of the Jewish people is known as the Diaspora.

During the Roman occupation of Judah, events took place that gave birth to Christianity. Followers of Jesus Christ, who was himself Jewish, were at first basically a Jewish sect and considered themselves Jews. As these early Christians converted non-Jews to their faith, Christianity became less "Jewish" in outlook, character, and ceremony. Like Judaism, Christianity was a monotheistic religion, with a belief in one God. Unlike Judaism, however, Christianity grew around the belief in Jesus as the **Messiah**, with a direct relationship to God. Despite the belief of Jews and Christians in one God, this important difference in belief regarding Jesus as the Messiah contributed to hostility between the two groups.

The Christians also felt they had a particular grievance against the Jews—they believed it was Jewish authorities in

The Blood Libel

In about the twelfth century, a rumor began to spread around Europe that Jews were kidnapping and killing Christian children so that they could use their blood in the baking of matzo, the flat bread used on the holiday of Passover. No one knows who made the story up, but the "blood libel," as it came to be known, refused to go away. Over the next eight centuries, it would resurface again and again, thus proving how deep anti-Jewish prejudice was in Christian culture and how resistant that prejudice was to common sense or education. In April 1903, for example, the rumor swept through the Russian town of Kishinev. Mobs gathered, and approximately fifty Jews were killed.

In the 1920s and 1930s, the Nazis were eager to spread the blood libel. Their newspaper, *Der Stürmer*, frequently printed reports, complete with explicit drawings, of evil-looking Jews draining the blood from Christian children.

The Jews have suffered a long history of persecution and murder. This illustration from the Middle Ages shows Jews being burned alive in the German city of Cologne.

Jerusalem who had asked the Romans to execute Jesus. Over the next fifteen centuries of European history—a period in which Europe was dominated by the Christian Church and Christian beliefs—the cry of "Christ-killers" would be heard whenever Christians turned on their Jewish neighbors. This happened quite often. For example, Christian armies set off from western Europe on the first **First Crusade** in 1096 to regain the Holy Land from the mostly Muslim Ottoman Turks. They made sure to kill any Jews they came across on the way.

Throughout this period, Jews were expelled from one European nation after another. They were usually allowed to return eventually, but sometimes only after centuries had passed. England, for example, expelled its Jews in 1290 and did not let them return until 1655. Spain expelled its Jews in 1492.

Wherever they lived, the Jews were on the edges of society. They were often forced to live together in small districts, or ghettos. (The word *ghetto* comes from one such district of Venice, Italy.) Sometimes they were made to wear distinctive clothes or symbols. Their religion, and the ways of living that went with it, set them apart. Increasingly, so did the jobs they took. Money-lending, in particular, became a common Jewish occupation because Christians were forbidden by their religion from engaging in it. Money-lenders might have been necessary, but they were rarely popular. Encouraging the Jews to become money-lenders provided the Christians with a service they wanted and also allowed them to despise the Jews for providing it.

This anti-Semitic cartoon from 1868 shows a Jewish money-lender. His money-tree is watered by gold and overdue debts.

The Eternal Scapegoat

The fact that the Christian majority used ideas related to their religion (such as calling the Jews "Christ-killers") as excuses for turning on the Jews does not mean that their motivation was always—or even often—truly religious. Throughout human history, people have looked for others to blame when things have gone wrong. In addition, those who really were to blame have tried to shift the responsibility onto others, who would be punished in their place.

Those wrongly blamed for accidents or other people's mistakes are called **scapegoats**. European Jews, as a small and visible minority, were constantly used in this way. When, for example, the Christian Church failed to protect its followers from plague, or a government failed to prevent an economic depression, it was always easier to blame the Jews than to admit to ignorance or mistakes. Church and government authorities encouraged ordinary people to take out their anger on the local Jewish minority, to expel or even kill Jews in the mistaken belief that such action would make things better.

A New World

The European Enlightenment movement, which began in the mid-seventeenth century and lasted until the early nineteenth century, marked a major change in the relationship between Jews and Christians in Europe. The followers of the movement tended to distrust all religions. They wanted people to respect each other as equal human beings, regardless of which God they worshiped, or whether they worshiped at all. The American and French Revolutions of the late eighteenth century tried, with some success, to turn these ideas into reality, and by the early nineteenth century, most of western Europe had come to accept them, at least in principle.

Martin Luther (1483–1546)

Martin Luther is a key figure in Christian history. Ordained as a priest, he later became professor of religion at the German University of Wittenberg. Luther led a revolt against the ideas and practices of the western Christian Church that brought about the Reformation (the division of the Church into Catholic and Protestant sections).

Luther became very anti-Jewish when Jews failed to convert to Protestantism, as he had hoped they would. In *On Jews and Their Lies* (1543), he advised Christians to set **synagogues** on fire, "and whatever does not burn up should be covered or spread over with dirt so that no one may be able to see a cinder or stone of it." Jewish homes should be "broken down or destroyed," and the Jews themselves made to "realize they are not masters in our land." Jews, Luther said, should be stripped of their belongings, "which they have dishonestly taken from us," and driven out of the country "for all time."

One consequence of these new attitudes was an end to the job restrictions that had long been placed on Jews. In western Europe, Jews were now free to become doctors, lawyers, journalists, or whatever they wanted to be. In theory at least, they had the same rights and opportunities as anyone else. This was not the case in eastern Europe, where many Jews had moved during the last few hundred years. There, job restrictions were mostly kept in place, and the Jews remained a group apart.

There was still a frequent need for scapegoats in both eastern and western Europe. The Jews, as Europe's only significant minority, still suited that role better than anyone else. The eighteenth and nineteenth centuries were also a time of rising **nationalism**, and in moments of crisis, it was all too easy for non-Jews to cast doubt on the loyalty of their Jewish neighbors.

"The Protocols of the Elders of Zion"

In August 1903, a Russian newspaper began printing a series of articles called "The Protocols of the Elders of Zion." These articles, which the paper claimed had been discovered by the Russian secret police, were said to contain a record of what Jewish leaders had said to each other at the first Zionist Congress in 1897 (see page 15). According to the "Protocols," the Jewish leaders had discussed their intention to take over the world. They supposedly planned to create hostility and distrust among other nations and mount a worldwide terrorist campaign.

The Russian czar gave medals to the secret policemen who had "uncovered" the plot, and book versions of the "Protocols" were published. Many people, however, were already claiming that the "Protocols" had been faked, and a government investigation discovered that they had actually been written by members of the Russian secret police. Unfortunately, this fact was not widely publicized. Many people, in the 1930s and even later, continued to believe that the "Protocols" were true.

Many Jews who came to the United States to avoid persecution in Europe settled in New York City's Lower East Side, shown above in about 1900.

After all, some nationalists argued, weren't the Jews different? Weren't they loyal to their own people first and to the nation second? Were they, perhaps, in secret contact with Jews who lived in other nations?

The Enlightenment period coincided with the **Industrial Revolution** and the growth of an often badly treated working class. Many of these workers formed **socialist** and communist parties to fight for greater equality, and many of their leaders were Jewish. Almost two thousand years of persecution had given the Jews a unique insight into life at the bottom of the social pile.

Approaching the Twentieth Century

What could the Jews do about their continuing persecution? Many thought that time was on their side, that the ideals of the Enlightenment would slowly spread. They thought societies would grow more tolerant, and differences of religion, culture, and nationality would become less important.

Alfred Dreyfus (second from right) is pictured here with General Gillain (center) and Captain Targe (center right), after the ceremony in 1906 in which he was forced to return his medals and resign his commission in the French army.

Other Jews were more pessimistic, and their views were reinforced by an outburst of anti-Semitism in France, known as the Dreyfus Affair. In 1893, Alfred Dreyfus, a French army officer who was Jewish, was wrongly accused of selling military secrets to a foreign power. There was no real evidence against him, and it is unlikely that he would have been found guilty had he not been Jewish. (Dreyfus was later acquitted and released from prison, and in 1906 he was reinstated in the army.) The Dreyfus Affair confirmed the fears of those who worried about the status of Jews in Europe: If there was this much prejudice in enlightened France, the pessimists argued, there was little hope of equal rights for Jews anywhere else in Europe.

Some Jews decided that it was time to give up the struggle for acceptance in other peoples' societies. It was time to build a society of their own, on their own territory. **Zionism**, the idea of recreating a Jewish state, was born. Palestine, the original home of the Jewish people, was the favored option, but many early Zionists were prepared to accept whatever homeland they could get.

As the nineteenth century came to an end, Europe's Jews had reasons for both hope and fear. Many Jews in western Europe now lived successful and prosperous lives, but prejudice lingered on and was always likely to deepen whenever a scapegoat was wanted. In eastern Europe, where the majority of the continent's Jews now lived, there were still ghettos, persecution, and even occasional **pogroms**.

Zionism and the Arab Response

Zionism—a movement to reestablish the Jewish nation, either in Palestine or wherever else proved practical—was a late nineteenth-century response to renewed persecution of European Jews, particularly in Russia. The movement's first leader was Theodor Herzl. In 1897, he organized the first Zionist Congress, a meeting to promote the Zionist movement, in Switzerland.

At that time, Palestine was part of the Turkish Ottoman Empire, but twenty years later, it became one of the battlefields of World War I. The Turks were driven out by the British, and in 1917, Zionism's second great leader—Chaim Weizmann—persuaded the British foreign secretary, Arthur Balfour, to support the idea of a national homeland for the Jewish people in Palestine. After the war ended, Jewish **emigration** to the territory increased.

Arabs made up a majority of the population in Palestine. As the Jewish presence in Palestine grew and the creation of a Jewish state became more likely, Arabs in the region became increasingly alarmed and angered. The British, who had effectively promised the same country to both peoples, were forced to limit the number of Jewish arrivals. Palestine would remain a possible safe haven from Nazi persecution, but one that was available to only a small portion of Europe's Jews.

CHAPTER TWO

The Rise of Germany Before World War I

A German Crime

The Holocaust was essentially a German crime. It is true that many citizens of other nations helped, either actively or passively, in the murder of six million Jews, and many Germans did not know what was going on. It was a German government, however—one supported by the majority of the German people— that ordered and executed this crime against humanity.

The New Germany

The Germans have a long history and a sense of themselves as a people that stretches back at least one thousand years. A unified German state, however, came into existence only in 1871, after one German state, Prussia, had won crushing wars over those neighbors—Austria and France—that had tried to keep the German peoples divided and weak. This Prussian success had several important consequences: an exaggerated respect for the military in the new Germany, an intense nationalism, and a dramatic speeding up of the new country's economic development. In 1870, the German economy was still based mainly on agriculture, but by 1900, Germany had overtaken Britain as Europe's biggest industrial power.

This combination of economic success and nationalistic pride had another consequence. Germany had joined the ranks of the great powers late, and Germans felt that, in some sense, they had missed the boat. Other great European powers— Britain, France, and Russia—had divided up most of the non-European world among themselves, and many Germans felt that now there should be some rearrangement of the globe that

By the early 1900s, Germany's economic growth and rapid modernization had turned it into the world's second largest industrial power, after the United States. This print shows a German iron foundry in 1900.

reflected Germany's growing importance. Their attempts to make this happen would be a major cause of World War I.

Germany against the World

The frantic economic growth that took place in Germany between 1870 and 1914 involved a vast expansion of the country's towns and cities. Political power, however, remained with the Kaiser (the German emperor), the old **aristocracy** of large rural landowners, and the military. As it grew more powerful, Germany also became increasingly divided.

Democratic government might have allowed Germany to work its way gradually from one type of society to another, but its elected parliament, the *Reichstag*, had little power. Those who did have the power were not prepared to share it. Instead, they tried to buy the support of working- and middle-class Germans in two ways. They introduced benefits such as state pensions and unemployment pay. They also promoted the idea that all Germans were united against the rest of the world.

Theories of Racial Superiority

Many wide-ranging theories about the pattern of human history merged from nineteenth century Europe and North America. One popular theory was to see history as an ongoing struggle for superiority among different races. The French philosopher Joseph Arthur Gobineau expressed this view in 1853 in "Essay on the Inequality of Human Races."

German philosphers seized on an idea known as "Social Darwinism," which put forward the theory that human history was all about the survival of the strongest races. Some of the German philosophers, such as Friedrich Wilhelm Nietzsche, were subtle and original thinkers, but that didn't stop people from reading whatever they wanted to read into the philosophers' ideas. When Nietzsche talked of masters and slaves, some Germans automatically assumed that they were the masters. Houston Stewart Chamberlain's book *The Foundations of*

Social Darwinism

In his 1859 book *On the Origin of Species*, British naturalist Charles Darwin proposed his now widely accepted theory of evolution. Natural history, he argued, was an endless struggle for living things to evolve, or adapt to changing circumstances. Those species that failed to adapt became extinct.

In the years that followed, philosophers known as Social Darwinists took Darwin's ideas and applied them to human society. Human history, they said, was also an eternal struggle in which only the strongest nations and races survived. This theory became particularly popular among Germans at the end of the nineteenth century. Social Darwinism not only rationalized an aggressive pursuit of German interests, but it undermined those who argued for moderation. If Germany failed to seize every advantage it could, the Social Darwinists argued, then the nation would go the same way as a failed species.

Richard Wagner
(1813–1883)

Today, Richard Wagner is most famous as a writer of classical operas such as *The Ring of the Nibelungs* (popularly known as *The Ring Cycle*) and *Tristan and Isolde*. During his lifetime, however, he was also well known for his political views, which were both intensely nationalistic and extremely anti-Semitic. The emotional appeal of Wagner's music and his nationalism probably influenced many Germans.

When the middle-class German revolution of 1848 was defeated, Wagner decided that the Jews were to blame. Their bad influence, he thought, had weakened the spirit of the German nation. Looking further, he decided that the Jews lay behind other problems too. In one essay entitled "Judaism in Music," he claimed that the Jews, were destroying all artistic endeavor by trying to make a profit out of everything. He further argued that because the Jews' true language was Hebrew, they couldn't speak any other nation's language well enough to share the soul of that nation.

Wagner's influence was widely felt. One of his disciples, Wilhelm Marr, invented the term *anti-Semitism* to describe dislike of Jews. Marr's British-born son-in-law, Houston Stewart Chamberlain, wrote the anti-Semitic book, *The Foundations of the Nineteenth Century*, which influenced Adolf Hitler. And Hitler shared Wagner's ideas and loved his music above all other.

the Nineteenth Century (1899) argued that Jews were an evil race set on world domination. It presented many of the arguments that Adolf Hitler would later use in his book *Mein Kampf*.

During the final decades of the nineteenth century, many anti-Semitic political parties appeared in Germany. Although they never did very well—winning only 4 percent of national votes at their peak—the parties were a sign of things to come. German Jews were aware of this anti-Semitic minority among their fellow Germans and hoped it would remain a minority. There were about 400,000 German Jews at this point—or just more than 1 percent of the population—and most of them believed that Germany offered them as civilized a home as they could hope for anywhere.

The Slide into War

The growth of German nationalism also had serious consequences for Germany's neighbors and the peace of Europe.

The leaders of Germany did not drag Europe into war on their own. Undemocratic governments in both Russia and Austria-Hungary were also trying to win popularity by being aggressively nationalistic. In addition, the fact that the great powers were tied together in a series of military alliances—somewhat like climbers roped together on a mountainside—also played its part. Between 1905 and 1913, there was a succession of international

This artist's impression shows the assassination of Archduke Franz Ferdinand by Gavrilo Princip in Sarajevo in June 1914.

On August 1, 1914, Germany declared war on Russia. When the news was announced in Munich, Adolf Hitler (circled) was in the crowd.

crises in which one power or another was forced by the threat of war to back down. Finally, in 1914, a crisis occurred (in relations between Austria-Hungary and Serbia) in which no one backed down. An event in Bosnia—the assassination of an Austrian archduke by a Bosnian Serb on June 28, 1914— set events in motion. Within weeks, Europe's five greatest powers—Germany, Russia, Austria-Hungary, France, and Britain—had pulled each other off the precipice and into what was soon referred to as "the Great War." This war was later known as World War I.

Germany went to war against Russia, France, and Britain with confidence. Germans fully expected the same sort of swift victories they had won in earlier wars against Austria (which had since become Austria-Hungary) and France. This was the chance Germany had been waiting for, the chance to gain the mastery that its size, strength, and industrial power deserved. The history of the German state was short, but it was a history of successes, and the German people expected more of the same.

CHAPTER THREE

World War I and the Fall of Germany

Defeat

Germany's hopes of success were ill-founded. Its resources and manpower had been inferior from the beginning. In addition, German military commanders had made grave mistakes. By 1918, their soldiers were weakened by death, sickness, and lack of food. Other nations that had fought with Germany against the Allies, such as Austria-Hungary, had been defeated, and the German effort was crumbling on several **fronts**. When large

The German army faced great difficulties in fighting against Russia in World War I. Above, German soldiers are hampered in their advance as they try to cross a body of water.

This map shows the changes made to European borders after 1919.

U.S. forces arrived in 1918 to reinforce the British and French armies on the western front, a German defeat was only a matter of time. German commanders pressed their government to agree to an **armistice**. Confronting a humiliating defeat, the German emperor, Kaiser Wilhelm, fled Germany on November 9.

The politicians who had led Germany during the war also vanished into the background, leaving the **Social Democrats** and other moderates to declare Germany a **republic** and set up a new system of government. On November 11, 1918, a German armistice commission accepted the Allies' peace terms. World War I was over.

The Weimar Republic

Germany's new regime, called the Weimar Republic, was in trouble from the start. Because almost all of the fighting in the war had taken place beyond Germany's borders, most Germans had no idea how badly things had gone in 1918. Shocked and angered by what seemed to them a sudden defeat, they demanded to know who was responsible. In addition, almost two million Germans had died in World War I, and a long naval

The Armenian Genocide

Up to ten million soldiers were killed in World War I, but compared to World War II, the number of civilian casualties was relatively small. The only government to carry out a mass murder of civilians was the Turkish government. The victims were members of Turkey's Armenian minority.

In 1915, while the rest of the world was distracted by the war, the Turks attacked the Armenians, murdering thousands in cold blood and driving the rest south toward the desert. By the end of the year, about 1.5 million Armenians had been killed. Most surprising of all, the Turks got away with it. After the war, the great powers of the West needed the Turks to help with the fight against communism, and they were not willing to upset them by bringing up the mass murder of the Armenians. This point was not lost on Hitler and the Nazis. Talking to his generals on the eve of World War II, Hitler reminded them that history always sided with the winner. To prove his point, he asked them a simple question: "Who still talks about the extermination of the Armenians?"

blockade had left millions more hungry and poor. Many German citizens felt an urgent and deep need for scapegoats.

Faced with this anger, the German military leadership—who had actually asked the government to end the war because they knew they were defeated—began claiming that they had been "stabbed in the back" by the politicians of the Weimar Republic. It was the new government, they said, that should bear the shame of defeat.

Many Germans realized that to blame the new government was nonsense, but others wanted their scapegoat. As the Republic stumbled from crisis to crisis over the next few years, more and more people chose to believe the lie. And as the severity and humiliation of the peace terms took their toll on Germany, the true reasons for defeat in the war were increasingly ignored or forgotten.

A Series of Disasters

The first crisis for the Republic was provoked by

German soldiers fought on the streets of Berlin during the failed communist uprising of 1918–1919.

the communists. In the early winter of 1918–1919, they seemed close to seizing power, but the Social Democrats and the German army combined to win a short and bitter civil war.

In 1919, the victors of World War I met in Versailles, France, to decide on the price that Germany would pay for its defeat. The U.S. president, Woodrow Wilson, wanted a fair settlement, one that would create a lasting peace. He based his proposals on the principle of self-determination, the idea that all peoples should be able to rule themselves. The French, however, were more interested in keeping Germany weak, and they got their way. The Treaty of Versailles gave 13 percent of Germany's territory to its neighbors and confiscated all its **colonies**. In addition, Germany's once-proud army was limited to 100,000 men and forbidden heavy weapons. Germany was forced to admit sole responsibility for starting the war and presented with a huge **reparations** bill. The defenseless Weimar Republic had no choice but to accept it all.

The burden of reparations soon led to another crisis— the Great **Inflation** of 1923. The need to pay reparations was crippling the German economy, and early in 1923, the Weimar government announced that it was suspending payments. The French retaliated by occupying the Ruhr, Germany's main industrial region. German workers then refused to work under French occupation, which further deepened the

economic crisis. The government printed money to help its people survive, but this succeeded only in creating runaway inflation. When prices of goods leaped higher and higher, wages leaped higher and higher to match them, until a whole suitcase of bills was needed to pay for a loaf of bread. There was hardship everywhere, and anyone with savings saw them wiped out.

German children played games with worthless banknotes during the Great Inflation of 1923.

Self-determination

In January 1918, U.S. president Woodrow Wilson outlined a fourteen-point peace plan for ending World War I. Many of his ideas, such as the creation of a new independent Poland, were based on the principle of self-determination, which stated that peoples should rule themselves rather than live in empires with rulers of another nationality. When the Germans agreed to the armistice terms in November 1918, they expected that this principle of self-determination would be applied to all nations, and they were dismayed to find that it would not apply to them. According to the territorial changes agreed to at Versailles, there would now be German minorities in several other nations, with particularly large groups in Czechoslovakia and Poland. Hitler and the Nazis would later claim that in demanding the return of territory from these states, they were only following Wilson's principle of self-determination.

The Usual Scapegoats

How did all this affect German Jews? In 1914, when World War I began, they had rushed to join the armed forces as eagerly as other Germans, and they were soon dying in similar numbers. When things started going wrong, however, Jews were quickly made the scapegoats. During the war, some anti-Semitic people had said that the Jews were not pulling their weight. They claimed that Jews were taking easy jobs behind the lines, rather than sharing the dangers of the front with "real" Germans. A government investigation proved that this was nonsense, but doubts had been raised.

Dr. Walter Rathenau was the German foreign minister in the early years of the Weimar Republic. A German Jew, he was murdered by anti-Semitic extremists in 1922.

Some people were eager to raise the doubts still further. They pointed to those Jewish businesspeople who had made money from the war, while ignoring the non-Jewish business-people who had made even more. They pointed out how many prominent communists were Jews, including political theorist and founder of communism Karl Marx and the German revolutionary leader Rosa Luxemburg, as well as many leaders of the Russian Revolution. They also pointed out that several of the leaders of the Weimar Republic—who had supposedly stabbed the army in the back—were also Jewish. Wasn't it obvious, the anti-Semites argued, that Germany had really been defeated by traitors within, by communists and Jews? As the Weimar Republic limped from disaster to disaster, more and more people began to believe this idea.

CHAPTER FOUR

Hitler and the Nazis

Adolf Hitler served four years with the German army in World War I. He is pictured (on the right) with two other soldiers and a dog at a German military hospital in 1918.

Adolf Hitler

Adolf Hitler was born on April 20, 1889, in the Austrian border town of Braunau, the fourth child of Alois and Klara. Alois Hitler, a fifty-one-year-old customs official of the Austrian Empire, retired when Adolf was six and died when he was almost fourteen. By all accounts, he was a hard and unsympathetic father. Klara Hitler, twenty-three years younger than her husband, died only a few years after him, in 1907. By this time, Adolf was living in the Austrian capital of Vienna. He wanted to study art but was twice rejected by the Vienna Academy of Fine Arts. Instead, he spent the next six years on the edge of poverty, doing odd jobs and painting postcards and posters to sell on the streets. He grew increasingly bitter that he, an Austrian German, was not doing as well as most of the Slavs and Jews around him. The longer he lived in Vienna, Hitler wrote later, the stronger his hatred became for what he called the "swarm of foreign peoples" who lived there. In the spring of 1913, having failed to register for the draft and fleeing to escape the Austrian authorities, he moved to Munich, Germany—the country for which his "heart had been secretly longing." He loved it there but was no nearer to finding a regular job when World War I began in August 1914.

Hitler joined the German army at once and served four years on the western front, mostly as a runner carrying messages between the fighting trenches and his unit's headquarters behind the lines. There seems no doubt that he enjoyed the war—it offered the friendships and sense of purpose that he had been unable to find in peace. He won medals for bravery and was hospitalized twice, once for a wounded leg and once for temporary blindness. He was still in the hospital when the war ended in November 1918. When he heard the news, he wrote later, "everything went black before my eyes." Unable to accept that the German army had been defeated, he convinced himself

Hitler in Vienna

"When home-going workers passed us by, Adolf would grip my arm and say, 'Did you hear, Gustl? Czechs!' Another time we encountered some bricklayers speaking loudly in Italian. 'There you have your German Vienna,' he cried indignantly. This, too, was one of his oft-repeated phrases: 'German Vienna,' but Adolf pronounced it with a bitter undertone. . . . He hated the clash of languages in the streets of Vienna . . . he hated this state, which ruined German-ness, and all those that supported this state: the royal family, the Church, the aristocracy, the **capitalists** and the Jews. . . . His accumulated hatred of all forces which threatened the Germans was mainly concentrated upon the Jews, who played a leading role in Vienna."

August Kubizek, who shared a room with Hitler in his Vienna days, in his book Young Hitler: The Story of Our Friendship (1953)

that it had been betrayed by the Weimar government who had accepted the peace terms. "During the nights," he wrote, "my hatred increased for the originators of this cowardly crime."

The Nazi Party

Hitler was not alone in thinking that something needed to be done to save Germany from the communists, socialists, and other "traitors" who, he wrongly claimed, had caused the defeat of the German army. In 1918–1919, many ex-soldiers formed units called *Freikorps* to take on communists in the vicious street battles that accompanied the brief uprising. Others started up extreme **right-wing** political parties. One of these, the German Workers' Party, was formed in Munich in 1919. Hitler

Alfred Rosenberg and the "Protocols"

Alfred Rosenberg (1893–1946) was born in Russia of German parents. He fought in the Russian army during World War I but fled to Germany after the Russian Revolution of 1917. Settling in Munich, he wrote articles claiming that the revolution was the result of a Jewish-communist plot. He also began working on a new edition of "The Protocols of the Elders of Zion." About this time, he joined the young Nazi Party and became friendly with Hitler. According to Rosenberg's explanation, the "Protocols" exposed the joint conspiracy between communists and Jews to destroy Russia and Germany. This involved setting the two nations at each other's throats and then reducing them to chaos through revolution. He argued Russia had already been destroyed, and Germany would be next if something wasn't done to destroy the communists and Jews.

Hitler liked the neatness of Rosenberg's theory. He later admitted that he knew the "Protocols" was a forgery, but he didn't care. What mattered, as Hitler saw it, was that the "Protocols" illustrated what he believed to be essentially true.

This is an artist's impression of Adolf Hitler speaking to fellow Nazi Party members during the years before the party came to power.

attended two meetings, agreed with most of what was said, and decided that the party was small enough for him to dominate. Within two years, he had become the party's leader. He gave it a new name: the *Nationalsozialistische Deutsche Arbeiterpartei* (National Socialist German Workers' Party), which was soon referred to in everyday usage as the Nazi Party.

Hitler drew up most of the policies of the party, which were all aimed at reversing Germany's defeat in World War I and punishing those held responsible for it. According to Hitler, the Treaty of Versailles would have to be scrapped and the land redistributed by the treaty returned. In fact, even more territory would be needed for Germany's growing population. Hitler argued that the German people could hope to succeed with such a program only if they were united under one leader. Nazi Party policy also said that those who encouraged disunity—the politicians of the Weimar Republic, the rich, the communists—should be denied any influence or power.

Adolf Hitler (center) and Alfred Rosenberg (left) were photographed during the failed Munich *Putsch* of 1923. Rosenberg published a new edition of the fraudulent "Protocols of the Elders of Zion."

According to Hitler and the Nazi Party, however, the greatest threat to German unity came from the Jews. They claimed that Jews were the power behind the scenes in the Weimar Republic, among both the rich and the communists. Moreover, Hitler said, there was no such thing as a German Jew. Only people of "German" blood should qualify for **citizenship**, he believed, and all noncitizens should leave the country.

Attempted Coup

In 1922, a right-wing politician named Benito Mussolini managed to overthrow the Italian government with not much more than the threat of a violent march on the capital, Rome. His success encouraged Hitler to try the same in Munich in 1923,

Early Nazi Intentions Toward the Jews

In February 1920, the Nazi Party issued a twenty-five-point statement of political policies. The following were points four through six. They look forward to denying the Jewish population all rights and opportunities in Germany and to preparing the ground for their expulsion:

- None but those of German blood, whatever their beliefs, may be members of the nation. No Jew, therefore, may be a member of the nation. None but members of the nation can become citizens, and so Jews cannot be citizens.
- Anyone who is not a citizen of Germany may live in Germany only as a guest.
- The right to vote on leadership and laws is to be enjoyed by citizens alone. All official appointments, of whatever kind, shall be granted to the citizens of the state alone.

when the Great Inflation was creating hardship across Germany. Hitler's Munich *Putsch* (or revolt), however, was resisted by the army. Sixteen Nazis were killed and Hitler was arrested for treason. He could have been sentenced to life in prison, but sympathetic judges decided he was a misguided patriot and gave him only five years in Landsberg, one of Germany's more comfortable prisons. He was released after only a year, having spent most of his time writing a book, *Mein Kampf (My Struggle)*.

Hitler's Vision

In his book, Hitler outlined his vision of Germany's future under Nazi leadership. The Treaty of Versailles would be torn up, Germany's lost territories reclaimed, and its colonies given back. He emphasized the struggle against communism and his determination to win more living space (*Lebensraum*) for the German people in the east by destroying the communist Soviet Union (the former Russian Empire). An extraordinary amount of *Mein Kampf*, however, was given over to Hitler's obsessive and extreme anti-Semitism. In his view, the Jews were the root of all evil, "maggots" who infected all decent societies the way they had infected the Vienna of his youth. He claimed that "a few Jews" had been responsible for Germany's defeat in 1918, and that the Jews as a whole were determined to "pollute" the blood of all other races.

Hitler's vision of Jews was, of course, a complete fantasy. So, too, was the "**Aryan**" master race—blond, blue-eyed, and Germanic—that Hitler believed he represented and that he believed fate had chosen to destroy the Jewish menace. According to Hitler, the future of civilization rested on the outcome of the struggle between these two races, a struggle that would need to be fought without mercy. In a letter written in 1919, he demanded the "complete removal of the Jews," though whether from Germany or the planet he did not make clear.

A Change of Direction
During his months in prison, Hitler changed his mind about the political tactics that he thought his Nazis should use. Rather than try to seize power by force, he decided to use legal methods, to build up the Nazi Party until it had won sufficient votes to form the government. He believed there were enough embittered Germans to make this possible.

Hitler's Hatred
"At the beginning of [World War I], or even during the war, if twelve or fifteen thousand of these Jews who were corrupting the nation had been forced to submit to poison-gas, just as hundreds of thousands of our best German workers from every social stratum and every trade and calling had to face it in the field, then the millions of sacrifices made at the [battle] front would not have been in vain."

Adolf Hitler, in his book Mein Kampf (My Struggle) Volume 2:
The National Socialist Movement *(1927)*

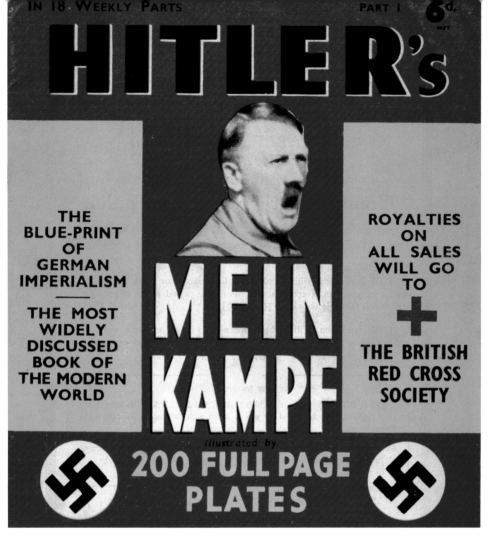

HITLER's

THE
BLUE-PRINT
OF
GERMAN
IMPERIALISM

———

THE MOST
WIDELY
DISCUSSED
BOOK OF
THE MODERN
WORLD

MEIN
KAMPF

Illustrated by
200 FULL PAGE
PLATES

ROYALTIES
ON
ALL SALES
WILL GO
TO

+

THE BRITISH
RED CROSS
SOCIETY

This is the front cover of the first part of the English edition of Hitler's *Mein Kampf*.

When released from prison, Hitler found that things had changed considerably. The Republic's government had managed to end the Great Inflation, and the other great powers had finally realized that a bankrupt Germany would be unable to pay any reparations. A German economic recovery was in everyone's interest, and, under the 1924 Dawes Plan, a series of mostly U.S. loans were arranged to get Germany back on its feet. The years 1924–1929 were good ones for all the developed countries of the world, including Germany, and parties like Hitler's, which relied on people feeling angry and desperate, found it hard to attract support. When the economic situation worsened again, however, they would be ready to step in.

CHAPTER FIVE

The Rise of the Nazis

Gathering Support

In May 1924, the Nazis and their sympathizers within the government won 6.5 percent of the vote in national elections. In new elections later that year, in December, their vote dropped to 3 percent, and throughout the next five years it remained at about this level. There was little demand for the Nazi Party's extreme policies while Germany was doing well.

Hitler and his party were not idle, however. Over these years, they formed Nazi organizations for all sorts of groups, from lawyers to teachers and students to businesspeople. Meetings

City Without Jews

As anti-Semitism grew popular in Germany and Austria, one Austrian Jew expressed his contempt by writing a novel in 1922. In *City Without Jews*, Hugo Bettauer imagined what would happen if the anti-Semites had their way and expelled the Jews from his hometown of Vienna. At first, the non-Jews celebrate, but soon they begin to notice unwelcome changes. Theaters go bankrupt, department stores close down, and cultural life fizzles out. Without their traditional enemy, the anti-Semitic parties lose their reason to exist. Realizing their "mistake," the people of Vienna invite the Jews to return.

The novel sold one-quarter of a million copies in its first year, a huge number for that time, and the Nazis were furious. A young Nazi named Otto Rothstock walked into Hugo Bettauer's office and shot him dead. Put on trial for murder, Rothstock emerged as a popular hero.

Germany was badly hit during the early years of the Great Depression. This photograph shows hopeful Germans holding out identity cards at an employment agency in Berlin where they were seeking work.

were used to spread Nazi ideas, and groups were encouraged to campaign against Jews in their line of work. Why was it, the Nazis asked, that Jews provided a full 16 percent of the country's lawyers and 11 percent of its doctors? Why did they own most of the big department stores? Such success, the Nazis implied, could only have been achieved dishonestly.

Nazis tried hard to attract young people to their party. The activities they organized, particularly for boys, were extremely popular. Between war games, patriotic songs, and stories of German heroes, Nazi leaders fed the young with the party's distorted version of German history and fantasies of racial purity.

Crash and Depression

If Germany had remained prosperous, it is hard to believe that the Nazis would ever have become more than a poorly supported party, screaming racial hatred from the sidelines. Like the rest of the world, however, Germany did not remain prosperous.

In October 1929, the price of shares on the New York stock market in the United States suddenly collapsed. The stock market crash swiftly led to the **Great Depression**, a worldwide slowdown of economic activity that threw millions out of work and lasted well into the mid-1930s.

Germany was particularly hard-hit. Loans from U.S. banks had kept the country going for five years, but these banks, now struggling themselves, demanded their money back. All over Germany, businesses went bankrupt. Between 1929 and 1932, the number of unemployed people rose from 1.3 million to 6.1 million. Once again, there was anger and confusion, and once again a cry for change. The Weimar Republic, and the moderates who made up its governments, seemed discredited, but what or who could take its place?

Hitler Gets the Call

As the moderates lost support, the extremists of both left and right won an ever-increasing share of the votes. The Nazi Party took 18.7 percent of the vote in September 1930. They doubled that total in July 1932, winning more seats in the *Reichstag* than any other party. The Communist Party also enjoyed large surges in popularity, and fights between supporters of the two parties became common on the streets of German cities. It seemed as

A huge crowd celebrated Hitler's appointment as chancellor outside the Presidential Palace in January 1933.

if the country was descending into violent chaos. Who was best qualified to sort it out? Most of the working class supported the Social Democrats or the Communists, but these parties did not have much support elsewhere. The upper and middle classes had lost what little faith they had in the Social Democrats, and they feared the Communists and their desire for class war. Voters turned to the Nazis, who talked of unity, order, a bright future, and an end to the chaos. Certainly they were extreme, but to many people it seemed as if extreme measures were needed.

After March 1930, when no party had managed to win an overall majority in the *Reichstag*, the **chancellor** was chosen by Paul von Hindenburg, then president of the Weimar Republic, and his **conservative** friends. They dreamed of a return to the sort of prewar Germany they had known in their youth, and they distrusted Hitler. The economy kept getting worse, however, and the fear of a communist revolution eventually persuaded them that Hitler was the lesser evil. In January 1933, Hitler, as leader of the largest party in the *Reichstag*, was finally appointed chancellor by von Hindenburg.

Who Voted for the Nazis?

The following is a list of some of the people who voted for Hitler:
- The traditional middle class, which had lost faith in the moderate parties and wanted an end to chaos;
- The upper classes, which feared a communist revolution and could think of no other way to prevent one;
- Small farmers and businesspeople, who had been bankrupted by the Great Depression or left behind by technological advances;
- Government workers and administrators, who feared losing their jobs;
- A younger generation excited by torchlight parades, violence, and the promise of dramatic change;
- Nationalists and anti-Semites.

CHAPTER SIX

The Nightmare Begins

The Jewish Reaction

Hitler's appointment as chancellor in January 1933 came as a terrible shock to most German Jews. "I had been skating that day," ten-year-old Leslie Frankel remembered years later. "When I got home we heard that Hitler had become chancellor. Everybody shook. As kids we shook." Some Jews decided to leave Germany as soon as possible. This group included many well-known artists, musicians, writers, and academics. Other Jews who were abroad at the time, like the famous scientist Albert Einstein, wisely chose not to return. Einstein instead emigrated to United States.

Stormtroopers

In 1921, the Nazi Party began recruiting bodyguards for their speakers at public meetings. These men, most of whom were ex-soldiers, were given brown shirts to wear and were called the *Sturmabteilung*—a word that means "storm section" and that was soon abbreviated to the initials **SA**. Its members were known as "**stormtroopers**."

After Hitler failed to seize power in 1923, the SA was banned, but it reemerged in 1926. Although its bodyguard duties had been taken over by a new black-shirted elite called the *Schutzstaffel*, or **SS**, the SA swiftly grew in numbers, from 2,000 in 1926 to almost 500,000 in 1933. During this period, the SA was mostly used to frighten political opponents and to fight the communists for control of Germany's streets.

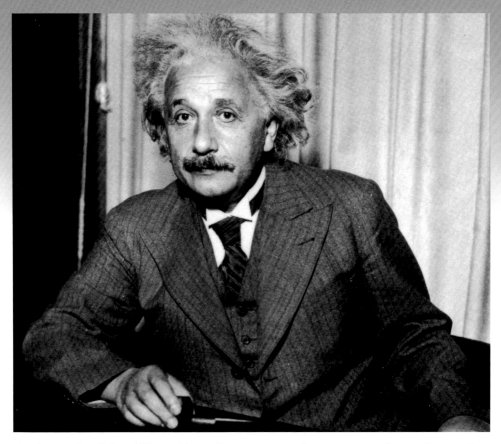

Nuclear physicist Albert Einstein was one of many prominent Jews who decided to leave Germany after Hitler's appointment as chancellor.

Most of the emigrants had money and talents they could easily make use of in another country. But emigration was not an easy option for most German Jews. Which country would take them in? Even if one or more nations agreed to do so, how could a family afford the fares and the cost of a home in a new country? More significantly, why should they leave Germany? Their ancestors had lived in Germany for hundreds of years, and German Jews felt themselves to be every bit as German as the Nazis. It was their home, and German was the language they spoke. They were reluctant to leave the lives they were used to. It would take more than a few isolated beatings by Hitler's stormtroopers to drive them out. After all, many German Jews told themselves, Germany was still a democracy, and the Nazis were only one party. If they sat tight, then the Nazi storm would surely blow itself out, and eventually things would get back to normal.

The End of Democracy

Hitler and the other Nazi leaders were aware that their position was far from secure. There were only two other Nazis in the **cabinet** beside Hitler, and although one of these, Hermann Göring, had a powerful position in charge of the country's police, any or all of them could be dismissed at any time by President von Hindenburg. What Hitler wanted was dictatorial powers. To gain such powers, he needed an enabling act, a law that allowed him to do what he wanted regardless of the president or the other parties. To get this enabling act, he needed a two-thirds majority in the *Reichstag*, and he had considerably less than half the votes. It seemed impossible.

But then, less than a month after Hitler became chancellor, the *Reichstag* building was burned to the ground. The man who was probably responsible—historians still disagree about this—was a Dutch communist named Marinus van der Lubbe. The Nazis claimed that his act was the signal for a communist campaign of terror. Other people claimed that the Nazis had started the fire to give themselves an excuse to turn on the communists. Either way, President von Hindenburg was persuaded to sign an emergency law suspending all civil liberties, restricting free speech, and allowing imprisonment without trial. Over the next few weeks, stormtroopers and the Nazi-controlled police arrested about ten thousand socialists and communists, including many members of the *Reichstag* who would have voted against the Enabling Act. When the vote was taken on March 23, 1933, the parties of the center supported the Nazis, and Hitler was given the power he wanted.

The day before, the first **concentration camp** was opened at Dachau, just outside Munich. A week later, the first anti-Jewish measures were introduced in Germany, barring Jews from working in a wide variety of occupations. The nightmare had begun.

Hermann Göring (1893–1946)

Hermann Göring fought as an army officer in World War I before transferring to the German Air Force and becoming a famous fighter ace. In 1922, he joined the Nazi Party, and in November 1923, he managed to escape abroad after being wounded in the party's attempted seizure of power.

Göring returned to Germany a few years later and was one of the Nazi Party's twelve successful candidates in the 1928 elections to the *Reichstag*. Over the next five years, he became Hitler's right-hand man in the party and his spokesman in the *Reichstag*. When Hitler was made chancellor in 1933, Göring became Prussian minister of the interior, which gave him control over Prussia's police force, Germany's largest. In the struggle against the communists that year, he told the police that they would not be questioned if they mistakenly used their guns, but they would be punished if they mistakenly failed to do so.

In later years, Göring commanded Hitler's new German air force and ran the German economy. After World War II, he committed suicide in his prison cell by taking some poison shortly before his scheduled execution for war crimes.

Time Line

922 B.C. Original Jewish state is established in ancient Palestine.

A.D. 66–73 Jewish rebellion against Roman rule fails in Palestine.

1096 Christian armies of First Crusade mass murder German Jews.

1290 Jews are expelled from England.

1492 Jews are expelled from Spain.

1543 Martin Luther's *On Jews and Their Lies* is published.

c. 1650–1900 Enlightenment period.

c. 1750 Industrial Revolution begins.

1853 Gobineau's "Essay on the Inequality of Human Races" appears.

1859 Darwin's *On the Origin of Species* appears.

1870 Prussian victories over France and Austria.

1871 Germany is unified.

1879 Term "anti-Semitism" is invented by Wilhelm Marr.

1889 April 20: Adolf Hitler is born in Braunau, Austria.

1893 Alfred Dreyfus is wrongly accused of selling French military secrets.

1897 First Zionist Congress is held in Switzerland.

1899 Chamberlain's *The Foundations of the Nineteenth Century* is published.

1903 April: Fifty Jews are killed in Russian town of Kishinev.
August–September: "The Protocols of the Elders of Zion" is printed in a Russian newspaper.

1914–1918 World War I.

1915 About 1.5 million Armenians are murdered in Turkey.

1917 Russian Revolution.
British Foreign Secretary supports the idea of a Jewish homeland in Palestine.

1918 German emperor abdicates.

1919 January: German Workers' Party is established in Munich.
May: Treaty of Versailles is signed.

1921 Nazi Party creates *Sturmabteilung* (SA).

1922 Bettauer's *City Without Jews* is published.
Mussolini's Fascist Party comes to power in Italy.

1923–1924 Great Inflation cripples German economy.

1923 Hitler is arrested during failed Munich *Putsch*.

1924 Hitler writes *Mein Kampf* in prison.
U.S. loans made to Germany in Dawes Plan.

1929 October: Stock market crash ushers in worldwide Great Depression.

1929–1933 Nazis become Germany's most popular political party.

1933 January: Hitler is appointed chancellor of Germany.
March: Nazi dictatorship is established in Germany.
Persecution of Jews inside Germany begins.

Glossary

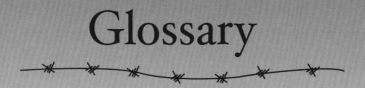

allies: people, groups, or nations that agree to support and defend each other. "The Allies" were the nations that fought together against Germany in World War I and World War II.

anti-Semitism: prejudice against Jews.

aristocracy: group of people who inherit by birth a high social rank or membership in a ruling elite.

armistice: agreement to stop fighting made between two sides in a war.

Aryan: according to the Nazis, a superior section of the white race, often distinguished by blue eyes and blond hair.

cabinet: group of officials, usually consisting of government department heads, that advises the head of a government.

capitalist: person who makes money from his or her existing capital (such as land, machinery, or money) or who favors the economic system of capitalism, under which there is private or corporate ownership of goods.

chancellor: executive head of the German government.

citizenship: rights, duties, and privileges associated with officially belonging to a nation.

civilian: person who is not serving in the military.

colony: territory owned or controlled by another nation.

communist: person who believes in the principles of communism, a political system in which the government owns and runs the nation's economy. (A Communist with a capital "C" is a member of the Communist Party.)

concentration camp: prison camp set up by the Nazis to hold Jews and other victims of the Nazi regime. Many prisoners held in these camps were never tried or given a date of release.

conservative: person who resists change and wants to preserve traditional ways in political, economic, and social systems.

democratic: based on a government system in which people vote on decisions or elect representatives to vote for them.

emigration: leaving one's own country to go and live somewhere else.

extermination camp: place set up by Nazis in which they murdered large numbers of people.

First Crusade: first of several wars in which European Christians fought Muslims for control of the Holy Land.

front: area in which battles take place. A front can move as one army advances and the other retreats.

genocide: deliberate murder or attempted murder of a whole people.

Great Depression: period of world-wide economic hardship that began in late 1929 and lasted through most of the 1930s.

Gypsy: member of a group that includes the Roma and Sinti peoples, who live mostly in Europe. Gypsies are traditionally nomadic, meaning they move from place to place.

homosexual: person attracted to others of the same sex.

Industrial Revolution: period in which an agricultural economy changes into one based on manufacturing. In Germany, the Industrial Revolution began in the early to mid-1800s.

inflation: increase in amount of circulated money that causes a steep rise in prices.

Judaism: religious culture of the Jewish people that centers around a belief in a single, divine intelligence.

labor camp: camp in which prisoners are forced to perform hard labor.

Messiah: leader and savior.

Middle Ages: period of European history from about A.D. 500 to 1500.

nationalism: active promotion of national interest, often at the expense of other nations.

pogrom: massacre of innocent people.

reparation: payment to make amends for damage caused by war.

republic: nation that is led by elected officials and that has no monarch.

right-wing: conservative in outlook and favoring national interests over those of humanity as a whole.

SA: short for *Sturmabteilung*, the Nazi private army also known as "the brown-shirts."

scapegoat: person unfairly blamed for misfortunes, mistakes, or wrongdoings.

Social Democrats: moderate socialist party in Germany that dominated the early years of the Weimar Republic.

socialist: person who believes in socialism, a set of ideas that emphasizes the needs of the community as a whole rather than the freedoms or needs of the individual.

SS: short for *Schutzstaffel*, a Nazi elite force also known as "the blackshirts."

stormtrooper: member of the SA.

synagogue: Jewish place of worship.

terrorist: person who performs acts of violence in order to make a political point or force a change in government policy.

Zionism: movement to reestablish a Jewish state in the Holy Land.

Further Resources

Books

Altman, Linda Jacobs. *Hitler's Rise to Power and the Holocaust* (The Holocaust in History). Enslow Publishers, 2003.

Downing, David. *Fascism*. Heinemann Library, 2002.

Feldman, George. *Understanding the Holocaust*. UXL, 1998.

Shuter, Jane. *Prelude to the Holocaust* (The Holocaust). Heinemann Library, 2003.

Stuart A. Kallen. *The Nazis Seize Power, 1933–1939: Jewish Life Before the Holocaust*. Abdo & Daughters, 1995.

Taylor, David. *Adolf Hitler* (Leading Lives). Heinemann Educational Books, 2002.

Web Sites

The Holocaust: Crimes, Heroes and Villains
www.auschwitz.dk
Web site about those involved in the Holocaust, with biographies, poetry, photos, and more.

The Holocaust History Project
www.holocaust-history.org
Archive of documents, photos, and essays on various aspects of the Holocaust.

Holocaust Survivors
www.holocaustsurvivors.org
Interviews, photos, and sound recordings of survivors of the Holocaust.

The Museum of Tolerance's Multimedia Learning Site
motlc.wiesenthal.org
Educational Web site of the Simon Wiesenthal Center, a Jewish human rights agency.

Non-Jewish Holocaust Victims
www.holocaustforgotten.com
A site dedicated to the Nazis' five million non-Jewish victims.

United States Holocaust Memorial Museum
www.ushmm.org
Personal histories, photo archives, and museum exhibits of the Holocaust.

About the Author

David Downing has been writing books for adults and children about political, military, and cultural history for thirty years. He lives in Britain.

Index

Page numbers in **bold** indicate illustrations.

48